CELEBRATING·SOIL

story by
Aaron William Perry

art by
Yvonne Kozlina

Copyright © 2018 Aaron William Perry

All rights reserved. No part of this book may be reproduced in any form or by any electronic or mechanical means, including information storage and retrieval systems, without permission in writing from the publisher, except by reviewers, who may quote brief passages in a review.

First Printing July 2018

Printed in the United States of America

Celebrating Soil

ISBN: 978-0-9986294-3-8 (pbk)

ISBN: 978-0-9986294-4-5 (ebk)

Library of Congress Control Number: 2018907361

Earth Water Press, Denver Colorado

www.earthwaterpress.com

To book this author for a speaking engagement or workshop, contact y@yonearth.world

Hi Friends!

My name is Sophia, and I'm a honeybee. I love flowers, sunshine and rainbows. I'm so excited to join you on this adventure *Celebrating Soil*! Look for me in each picture—I'll be your friend and guide through the whole book!

We may encounter some new terms and concepts. Not to worry! The Y on Earth Community team has provided us resources at the back of the book to help answer questions and share some of their special knowledge and inspiration!

Are you ready for an adventure together?

Buzzing with Love,

Brother woke up very early this morning, just as the robins and sparrows were starting to sing their joyful song to greet the rising sun. The sky was getting light, and he could see the planet Venus leading the way just above the horizon. He knew the bright sun would soon follow and bring the daylight. Brother is so excited today!

Sister also woke up early today. Looking out the window in the other direction, she sees the full moon setting just as the sun is rising on the opposite horizon. She is also so excited this morning—just like Brother!

Today Brother and Sister are especially excited to go outside and play after breakfast!

Once outside, Brother and Sister see the kind old man with the white beard and his friend, the wise old lady with the long flowing hair, walking to their garden. Just as the old man and the old lady walk up to the gate, a colorful, shimmering hummingbird darts by, singing his special hummingbird wing song as he flies and hovers all around. It is so much fun to see the old man and the old lady—they're great friends—and magical things always seem to happen when they visit!

The old lady is carrying a basket of strawberries, carrots, and sweet, sweet snap peas and gives them to Brother and Sister who are now greeting them at the gate and welcoming them into the garden.

The old man and old lady are overjoyed to find Brother and Sister frolicking barefoot and playing in the dirt. They take their shoes off right away and join in the fun!

As they are all dancing and frolicking, playing under the blue sky and the bright sunlight, the old man crouches down at the edge of the garden and draws a circle on the ground. Then he scoops up a handful of dark, rich soil from within the circle.

"Do you know what this is?" he asks Brother and Sister with a glimmer in his eye.

"Dirt?" they respond together in unison.

"Yes, but not just any dirt!" the old lady chimes in as she joins the old man at the garden's edge. "This is sacred, living soil. Full of billions and billions of teeny tiny living organisms—micro-organisms—vibrating with life, magic, and mystery as they make the soil! And guess what? Each handful of this living soil contains as many living micro-organisms as there are people on the Planet—billions!"

"They are full of the life-force," the old man continues. "Have you heard of the life force before?" he asks Brother and Sister.

"Yeah, sort of," Brother replies.

"Maybe in a story or a movie," Sister adds.

"Yes, good," the wise old lady tells them. "The life force is talked about in many, many stories—by cultures and people all over the world and throughout time. Some people call it energy," she continues, "some call it light and some call it love."

She looks Brother and Sister directly in the eyes, as she speaks. "Whatever we call it, the life force is generated especially by the micro-organisms in the soil. Along with the sunlight and water, they help make all of the plants grow—including all of the strawberries, carrots, snap peas, and apples that we all eat and enjoy. As well as all of the flowers, trees, bushes, and grasses that are so beautiful and fun to play on too! They make our lives possible here on Planet Earth. Isn't that wonderful?" The old lady then springs up and starts dancing around in playful, spinning circles while laughing and singing.

Now, the kind old man is drawing a square within the circle. Oh, how he loves to draw shapes! At each corner of the square, he draws a special symbol and writes a special word: Soil, Water, Air, Sunlight. "These four elements," the old man told Brother and Sister, "flow through all of us in special, mysterious ways."

"The life force," continues the wise old lady, as she touches her finger, marking a dot in the center of the square, "is what animates the four elements with life! And, when we touch and hold the soil, the little organisms give us invisible nourishment that makes us feel good, by helping us produce a special substance called serotonin. It also makes our immune systems strong and it makes our bodies and minds healthy and full of good energy!"

Sister and Brother look at each other in amazement and then at the old man and lady with wonder and awe.

"And, it's the very same soil and life force that allows all of the trees to grow so large and strong—providing shade and shelter for so many creatures," she told them with a great big smile.

"Amazing!" proclaims Brother.

"How wonderful!" Sister cries out as she stands up and starts dancing with her bare feet on the soft grass and soil."

All of them—Brother, Sister and the old man and old lady—start laughing and dancing and celebrating—what joy to know about the living soil!

But then the kind old man sits down suddenly and looks sad for some reason.

"Yes, the living soil and the life force are so wonderful—they are a great gift of creation—but they have been badly, badly hurt by us humans. For a few generations now, we have been dumping and spraying chemicals and poisons all over the soil and plants . . . and have been killing the micro-organisms living there! It's so sad."

"No!" cries Sister.

"That isn't good!" Brother exclaims.

"No, it isn't good at all," agrees the old lady, "and it is time to stop the poisoning right now . . . before it's too late.

"You can start in your own garden and neighborhood. Making sure that everything you're doing with your soil is free of the harmful, poisonous chemicals. Making sure that it is organic, biodynamic, clean and safe—for you, your pets, and the little organisms growing and living in the soil. You, too, can learn to take great care of the soil, and become a member of the Soil Stewardship Guild! And then, you can tell your friends, and their parents and all of your neighbors about it as well—for the living soil needs all of us to take care of it!"

"I will!" pledges Sister. "I will take care of the soil and help others to do the same!"

"I will too!" echoes Brother.

Then the old man tells them, "You are now part of the Soil Stewardship Guild! You can help your parents, neighbors and friends learn about the fun and easy ways we can all become great stewards of the soil! By composting, shopping for organic and biodynamic food and sustainable clothing, and even by growing plants inside and outside! And, one of the most important things we can do is share a very special, probiotic medicine with the soil—Biodynamic Soil Activator. Biodynamic Soil Activator is like organic, homeopathic medicine for the soil, plants and trees—full of billions of beneficial micro-organisms! It is so much fun to stir and sprinkle all around the yard and neighborhood—you can do this with your friends and family!"

They all look at each other with purpose and commitment in their eyes. And to celebrate, the wise old lady passes around the basket and offers the strawberries, carrots, and snap peas. Sister is amazed at how sweet they taste. And Brother thinks to himself how wonderful that he could almost taste the mustiness of the soil, the freshness of the water, the purity of the air and the heat of the sunlight as he takes each bite.

The wise old lady smiles. The kind old man bows deeply. And they take their leave of the family and walk away hand in hand through the garden gate.

"Thank you," Brother calls after the old lady and old man. "Thank you for visiting us today and sharing all of this with our family."

"We will go now and share what you have taught us with other families," Sister says.

"Blessings to you all," the wise old lady sings out.

"And may the life force be with you!" the kind old man says as he looks back and winks at Brother and Sister over his shoulder.

The End

About the Y on Earth Community

Connecting with the Y on Earth Community provides you and your community powerful, accessible tools and hope-filled inspiration to enhance day-to-day health and well being while deeply aligning with global strategies for regeneration, stewardship and sustainability. Our simple and empowering tools for "Thriving"—in the domains of soil, food, nature, movement and well-being—are fun for children of all ages! Visit yonearth.org/kidscorner to continue your journey!

Use Biodynamic Soil Activator / Land Medicine in your Yard and Neighborhood!

A wonderful way to celebrate soil, water and community is to mix the powerful Biodynamic Soil Activator in a bucket of water, and stir with family and friends before sprinkling and spraying this probiotic goodness all over your yard and even in your neighborhood and nearby parks! This is a very special land-medicine prepared according to the methodology provided by Rudolf Steiner about 100 years ago! Visit yonearth.org/soilactivation to get started!

Calls To Action

Take these five easy steps in your home with your family. And, you can gently encourage your neighbors, friends, and places of work, worship and gathering to do the same!

1. **Stop Poisoning Your Place**—and you'll no longer expose soil microbes, honeybees, children, pets or other family and loved ones to these dangerous chemicals.

2. **Start Building Soil**—with the techniques outlined in the Soil Stewardship Handbook, you can embark on the fun, easy adventure of building soil and joining the Soil Stewardship Guild!

3. **Give Biodynamic Soil Activator**—to your yard, neighborhood, parks and friends and family! This is one of the most powerful ways we can spread living goodness throughout our communities.

4. **Gently Share**—with your neighbors, school-mates, co-workers and others. We are all in this together, and we all have opportunities to improve our health and well-being through soil stewardship!

5. **Take the Soil Stewardship Pledge**—it's on the next page for you to read and sign!

And check out the *Soil Stewardship Handbook* for even more great ideas and activities from the Y on Earth Community!

SOIL STEWARDSHIP PLEDGE

I, _____, believe that my connection with living soil is sacred. I promise to be a faithful steward of soil, and thus of Mother Earth—through my direct interactions with soil as well as the indirect influences of my personal choices and consumer demand. I promise to be mindful of my impact upon soil every day. I will compost all of my organic kitchen scraps and food waste. I will grow plants inside and a garden outside. I will touch soil with my hands every day. I will gently and joyfully encourage others to join our Soil Stewardship Guild. I will do all that I can to establish living soil installations at home, at work and elsewhere in my community. I understand that soil-building is a powerful way to reverse climate change. I understand that healthy, vibrant soil is key to nourishing food and clean water. I know that our existence as humans is dependent on soil. I vow to be an excellent steward and to help others to do the same.

_____
Signed

_____
Dated

_____
Acknowledged and Approved by Aaron William Perry
Author and Founder, *Y on Earth* and Soil Stewardship Guild

FIDES VIVI HUMUS
(Faith in Living Soil)

About the Author

Author and founder of the Y on Earth Community, Aaron William Perry is an entrepreneur, writer, speaker, consultant, and father. The author of *Y on Earth: Get Smarter, Feel Better, Heal the Planet,* Aaron works with the Y on Earth Community and Impact Ambassadors to spread the THRIVING and SUSTAINABILITY messages of hopeful and empowering information and inspiration to diverse communities throughout the world. He resides in Colorado where he loves to hike in the mountains, is continually in awe of the ever-changing weather, and entertained by the hilarious antics of his backyard, free-range (and free-thinking) chickens.

About the Illustrator

Yvonne Kozlina is a professional portrait artist and painter who originally hails from Pittsburgh, Pennsylvania and now makes Colorado her home. A mother and grandmother, She loves children and has taught art to diverse children of all ages. Yvonne's photo-realistic style is uncanny, as she taps in to the essence of the people she paints and draws. She is also an avid animal lover, gardener, and enjoys taking walks through the neighborhood when she isn't at her easel painting. See Yvonne's artwork and learn more about her custom portrait services at yvonnekozlina.com.

See you later!

www.ingramcontent.com/pod-product-compliance
Lightning Source LLC
Chambersburg PA
CBHW041435010526
44118CB00002B/80